I0428457

Random

Acts

Of Kindness

Donna and Arnie Gilson

DEDICATION

Our parents who taught by example

ACKNOWLEDGEMENTS

To all persons who have given any acts of kindness

CONTENTS

Single Mother gets groceries

....

He was in line with the few groceries he had picked up.

Just in front of him was a young cute petite lady, perhaps twenty-five or so with two young children. There was a little girl seated in the shopping cart who looked to be maybe two years old and a boy standing next to the cart. He looked like he might have been four.

He smiled at the little boy and gave a little wave. The boy acted bashful and hid behind his mother.

She looked back to see who was causing the shyness and gave a little smile.

To him, she looked a little sad and tired. He also noticed she was not wearing a wedding band so she must be a single mother.

He also noticed she was going though her money. He could see a twenty dollar bill, a five dollar bill and some ones. She seemed to be studying them closely.

When it came time for her to put her items

on the conveyor belt, he noticed she would put on a couple of items then wait to see how much she had spent to that point.

It was obvious that she was concerned she did not have enough money for all the items she had in her cart.

He turned around so she could not see him take a twenty dollar bill out of his wallet.

He turned back toward her and pretended to pick up something off the floor.

"I believe you dropped this," he said as he handed the bill to her.

She looked at the bill and at him with a puzzled look on her face.

He gave a little wink.

She knew what he had done and asked, "Are you sure?"

"Just saw it laying there by your feet," he said with a smile.

He could see the tears welling up in her eyes.

With out any hesitation, she loaded all the rest of the items on the conveyor belt knowing she would now have enough money to pay for all of them.

After the cashier had rung up the items and took the cash, she gave her the change. It was several dollars.

The young lady turned to him offering him the change.

He raised his hand with palms toward her as a sign he didn't expect it.

Again, the tears were welling up in her eyes and she left but was still looking back at her benefactor.

When he put his items on the conveyor, the cashier started scanning them and, with out looking at him said, "I saw what you just did."

"Don't know what you're talking about," he said.

As he left, he dropped off his cart in the cart foyer because he only had a couple of bags and then went out the automatic door onto the sidewalk.

The young lady and her two children were standing there as if waiting for him to come out.

They approached him and said, "I want to thank you for what you did in there. Here, please take the change," she begged.

He repeated what he had said to the cashier, "Don't know what you're talking about." Winked again, then turned and walked to his car.

He noticed the girl was wiping the tears from her eyes.

Mark Troyer had just committed a random act of kindness and it made his day. It wasn't the first time he had done a random act and most certainly would not be the last time

Jan Butler, the widow, her two children, Timmy and Betsy, also had good feelings.

She wished she had gotten his name.

Mark had learned about kindness from his father many years ago.

He remembered one time when there was a massive snow storm that had shut down the school for the day.

He was lying around watching the TV when his dad suggested that he take the snow shovel down to Mrs. Andrews, who was an aged widow, and shovel her side walks.

He said, "Don't let her know you did it and I guarantee you will remember that long after the memory of the TV program you're watching is forgotten."

Years later, Mark would think about his dad and thank God for the examples he had shown him as he was growing up.

****

A prom date gets a gown

....

Brandi Montgomery was hosting a slumber party for the five other member of the cheer squad. Brandi was the squad captain.

They all did the 'girly' things like do and re-do hair styles and give each other manicures and pedicures. There might have been a pillow fight or two.

A favorite topic at slumber parties is boys, boys and more boys. The most important topic that night was the Prom and who would be getting asked and by whom.

Two of the girls had 'steadies' and were assured of a date for the event.

The other four were waiting, impatiently, of course because the Prom was less that a month away.

The girls thought Brandi would surely be asked by Mark Anderson who was captain of the football team.

Seemed like a perfect match.

Problem was, Mark had not gotten around to giving Brandi an invitation.

Charlotte Anderson was eating breakfast with her brother, Mark when she asked, "Make a date for the Prom yet?"

"Not yet," he answered reading the box of cereal.

"You had better get around to it, it's only three weeks away and a girl has to make plans. "I'm sure you will be asking Brandi Montgomery," she continued.

"I don't think so," Mark said this time looking at his sister, "I don't really care much for her. Seems to be too much into herself," he added.

"With her looks and body, she has every right to be 'into herself'. I should be so lucky," she said trying to look at her reflection in her spoon.

Mark went on to say, "There's a girl in my English class that I really like, but when I asked her, she wouldn't give me an answer."

"So who are we taking about here?" Charlotte asked.

"Her name is Peggy Nash." Mark said with a smile.

"I think I know her. Does she have short blonde hair?" she asked.

"Yeah, that's the one," Mark answered.

"Doesn't seem to be your type," Charlotte teased.

"Don't know what my type is supposed to be, but I think she's really nice. She is also smart, probably gets the highest grades in the class."

"Well, don't give up bro. You would be a *great* catch for a prom date," she said as she got up to rinse her bowl.

Mark looked at her with a surprised look and Charlotte, herself, wondered why she said that about her brother, of all people..

As siblings, they were close.

At noon, Charlotte was going through the cafeteria line when she spotted Peggy Nash over in a corner almost by her self.

She went over and asked, "I know I'm only a junior and you're a senior, but mind if I join you?"

Peggy laughed and said, "I would consider it an honor."

Right away Charlotte now knew what her brother was seeing in Peggy.

"I'm Mark's sister," she told Peggy.

"I know, I've seen you two around quite a bit. I thought your were a couple because you seem so close," Peggy commented.

"Just an illusion. We are typical brother and sister with the usual sibling rivalry," she said with a smile.

"I under stand Mark has asked you to the Prom," Charlotte went on to say.

Peggy dropped her head and with a sigh, and got a sad look on her face.

Charlotte sensed something and asked, "Is there anything wrong?"

Peggy then told her the story............

The next Saturday morning, Charlotte was coming down the stairs carrying two of her gowns that had been stored in plastic garment bags.

Her mother stopped her and asked what that was all about.

"On a mission," she told her and asked for the keys to her mother's car.

Her mother thought with a smile, "That could be anything." She knew her daughter all too well.

Charlotte came back home about mid afternoon and knocked on Mark's door.

"You in there bro?" she hollered through the door.

"Yeah, deep into my math homework," he answered.

"Want you to do something for me – and for yourself," she continued to talk through the door.

"And what, exactly would that be?" he asked in a cautious tone.

"When you see Peggy in class on Monday, ask her again for a Prom date," she instructed.

Mark had his eyebrows pinched together in deep thought. "Why?" he asked.

"Just do it," she answered and walked away.

Mark was getting up enough nerve to approach Peggy, not knowing what to expect when he would "pop the question' about the prom.

When he asked her, she coyly said she would like that very much.

The rest of the day was lackadaisical for Mark. He felt in seventh heaven after Peggy's acceptance.

When he got home that afternoon, he confronted Charlotte asking her how she knew that Peggy would accept his invitation.

"Don't have the slightest idea what you're talking about," she said with a smirky smile and a tilted head.

"Well, I did what you said and Peggy accepted," he said, sounding relieved.

"How about that. Congratulations," she said.

Some how, Mark knew that Charlotte was involved in this some how.

The evening of the Prom, at last, arrived and found Mark outside Peggy's door dressed in a rental tux and with a corsage in a clear plastic box. A limo was parked at the curb.

Peggy's parents opened the door and greeted Mark with broad smiles.

He was ushered in and stood in the foyer waiting for Peggy.

It wasn't a long wait.

She came down the stair looking like a real princess. Marks heart did a flip flop.

"How did she become so beautiful and what a startling gown she was wearing," he almost said out loud. Or maybe he did.

They left, but not before Mark told Peggy's parents exactly when they could expect her home.

They liked this kid.

The Prom was a huge success.

Brandi Montgomery was there with the Co-captain of the football team. She could hardly believe her eyes when she saw Mark with Peggy. At first, she didn't recognize her because she turned out to be quite a beauty in that spectacular gown.

She hardly looked like the plain girl she had

been seeing around campus.

As promised, Mark had Peggy back home at the time he had told her parents. Again, they really liked this kid.

Turns out, Peggy couldn't accept Mark's earlier invitation because her father had recently lost his job and there was no extra money for a gown.

That was what Peggy had told Mark's sister at lunch that day

Charlotte Anderson knew exactly what she had to do. She took two of her gowns to Peggy's house that Saturday and, between the two, came up with that ever so special gown that Mark and everyone else had admired.

Charlotte also went over to Peggy's house the day of the Prom and did her hair and nails.

Again, the things that Mark had noticed about Peggy as she walked down the stairs.

Mark never knew, because Charlotte never told him. Perhaps some day.

* *

An elderly lady gets help

....

Nel Binghan was in her late sixties. She looked a lot older, feeble and bent over most of the time. Her life hadn't been a happy one by any stretch of the imagination.

She lost her husband, Everett over 25 years ago and has been alone all those years.

She had family but they were six hours away and were never a close knit family to begin with. So she rarely saw any of them.

Her modest bungalow was, at least, paid for, but the taxes, insurance, upkeep and utilities took most of her social security which wasn't all that much to begin with.

Her fifteen year old car had given up the ghost a number of months ago, leaving her practically isolated.

A couple of neighbors would let her ride along to the supermarket with them when they went, but that wasn't too often.

She mostly depended upon a convenience store four blocks away that she could walk to. The walk was always painful because of an arthritic condition she suffered.

Troy Peterson stopped by that particular convenience market one afternoon to pick up a gallon of milk his wife had told him to bring home.

It was easier and faster stopping there than going to a market.

That particular time, Nel happened to be there to pick up a few necessities.

Troy couldn't help noticing her because of her appearance. To him she looked so sad and he felt sorry for her.

He wondered what her story was.

When he checked out, he asked the clerk what she was all about. He shook his head slightly and told Mark as much about her sad story as he knew, that she lived up the street a few blocks and would walk down here at times for a few items.

Troy looked back at her again as he walked out the door.

He decided to wait until she came out to offer her a ride.

Nel came out of the store carrying her items in a worn out cloth shopping bag that had sturdy strap handles. She looked emotionless and sad.

Troy walked up to her and said, "I understand you live up the street a little bit. I'm going that way, may I give you a lift?"

She looked up at him with a slight smile and said, "That would be nice. It won't be out of your way, will it?"

"Not in the least," he told her, "It would be my pleasure."

Actually it was out of his way. Troy would have been going in the other direction.

Nel gave him a slight suspicious look wondering who this nice man was.

Never the less, she got in Troy's car as he held the door open for her.

Her little house was, if fact, four blocks away and when they got there Troy noticed a car in the drive.

"Yours?" he pointed out.

"Yes, but it doesn't run any more," she said with a sad look and a slightly bowed head.

For some reason, Troy had some real concerns.

He said, "That's just like the car I had in college. (It wasn't, but he was coming up with an idea). "Mind if I take a look?" he went on to say.

"If you would like," she said, "It's kinda gone to seed"."

Mark pretended to languish over the car

pretending to experience some nostalgic moments.

"Did you say you can't drive it?" he asked.

"It died a few months ago, bless its sole," she answered.

"Would you consider selling it?" he asked trying to put a hopeful look on his face.

"Why in the world would you want with that broken down piece of junk?" she asked back.

"As I said, it was just like the one I had in College so I might want to relive my past", he tried to explain.

With that, he pulled out his cell phone and got on a web site that would give what the car should be worth.

It came up $2,100.00, but that was if the car was average and, of course, running.

He showed the figure to Nel and said, "I'll give you what it's worth, $2,100.00.

Nel looked at the screen then up at Troy, then back at the screen and said, "It's not worth that much," she said.

"OK, then I will give you $2,000,00 and not a penny less," he said as he was smiling at her. "Tell you what," he went on, "I'll let you sleep on it and I will come back tomorrow to see if it is a deal, OK?"

Nel shook her head and said, "OK, I guess."

Troy walked her up to her door and saw that she got inside before he left. "See you tomorrow at ten." he said pretending to look with feeling toward the car.

At ten the next morning, Troy was at Nel's door with a smile on his face.

Nel opened the door with an expression that indicated to Mark that she really hadn't expected him back.

"Deal?" Troy asked.

"I suppose so, but I don't feel right taking so much money for it," she commented.

"Like I said yesterday, I won't give you any less than I told you, and that's final," he tried to sound demanding. .

He didn't give her any time to say anything else. He asked her what bank she used and they went to her closest branch and deposited $2,000.00 into her account.

He dropped her back to her home and told her that he would send someone over to pick up the car later.

"Wait a minute and I will get the title and papers

for you," she said as she hurried into the house.

"Don't worry about that now, we can do that anytime," He yelled back to her as he started for his car.

A few hours later, a tow truck came by, hooked up the car and hauled it away.

Several weeks later, Troy drove up with the car that have been completely restored to show room condition,

He went up to the door and asked Nel if she would like to see her car now.

She walked out of the door, stopped, and said, "Oh my goodness, it looks just like it did when I bought it years ago."

"Thought it might," Troy said, "Come over and take a closer look," as he took her hand and led her to the driver's side door.

He opened the door so she could see how the inside looked.

"It even smells like a new car," she said as she looked at it as if it was a new baby.

"Had a lot of fun working on it and brought back a lot of wonderful memories," He said. He was still sticking to the story that it was like the one he had long ago.

She stood back with an admiring look when Troy said, "Hold our your hand,"

She did as he told her and he dropped the keys in it and closed her fingers over them.

She looked up at him with wonderment on her face.

"It's yours." He said with a big grin on his face.

"Oh, by the way, I found your insurance agent's card in the glove compartment and renewed the insurance for the next two years. After that you are on you own", he continued as he handed her the receipt he had gotten from her agent.

Just then, as planned, Troy's wife drove up to give him a ride back to their home.

Nel suddenly noticed that Troy was starting for his car. "Wait! Wait!" she cried.

"Can't, gotta run," he yelled back, "enjoy."

Troy's wife, Evelyn gave him a big hug and kiss when he got to the car.

As they drove away, they looked back and gave a wave to a still stunned Nel.

Nel turned and looked at her treasure.

She seemed to be standing a little straighter.

A young girl sees life a little differently

....

Twelve year old Sarah Troyer was having a happy childhood. Her family was very close and typical Americana in every way,

It was a comfortable life and the examples she was exposed to would reflect in her being a very well adjusted pre teen.

Carole Hampton, a classmate of hers, was just the opposite.

Her family was what you might consider, dysfunctional.

Carole's father had abandoned the family when she was an infant leaving her mother and her siblings to lead a struggling life.

Carole never had the nice clothes that most of the other girls had and was often teased even to the point of being bullied.

One day at recess Carole was being teased relentlessly by some of the snobby girls.

When the recess was over, Sarah noticed that Carole had tears in her eyes.

That bothered her so, at that moment, she decided that she would try to get to be a friend to Carole.

After school, she cornered Carole and asked her if she would like to come over to her house for a play day.

Carole looked a little puzzled, but said she would ask her mother if she could.

Naturally, her mother had no objection, so plans were make for the next Saturday.

Sarah and her mother picked Carole up and that's when Sarah got a good look at where Carole was living.

Didn't look all that great, she was thinking to herself

Her mother, no doubt, must have been thinking the same thing.

Back at Sarah's house, Carole was admiring their surroundings. She really envied Sarah.

The two of them were in Sarah's bedroom doing all the girly things that twelve year olds do.

Sarah opened her closet and Carole got a good look at all the nice clothes that Sarah had.

Carole was not aware that Sarah and her mother had agreed before hand that she would give her some the clothes that she didn't really wear that often.

Sarah had Carole try on several outfits and if she noted an admiring look on Carole's face as she viewed herself in the mirror, she would make a mental note that would be one of the outfits that would go home with her.

At lunch, they were all gathered at the kitchen table which included Sarah's father, mother and her two brothers.

Sarah's father asked Carole where her father worked. Sarah's mother, who knew the family story, gave him a little kick under the table.

"Oh," her father said and let the subject drop.

Sarah noticed, as the day went by that Carole started to smile a lot, much more than she had ever noticed before.

Problem was, Carole would have to return back to her home and the reality of life as she knew it.

Sarah had been putting all the clothes she had chosen to give to her new friend, in a couple of shopping bags.

Carole didn't notice that she had been doing that.

When they went to leave, Sarah handed the bags to Carole and said, "Here, these are yours."

Carole looked at the bags, then at Sarah and almost burst out in tears.

Carole felt ten feet tall at that moment.

Sarah's whole family drove Carole home and her father walked them to the door.

They were greeted by Carole's mother who noted the two shopping bags full of clothes that she was carrying.

Rather puzzled, she introduced herself to Sarah's father and told him how much she appreciated the kindness they all had shown her daughter.

Sarah's father told Mrs. Hampton that he knew of a well paying job opening in his firm that she might possibly be interested in.

Of course, she was.

The future for the Hampton family was now to make a dramatic turn for the better.

Sarah and Carole became fast friends that lasted for many, many years, thanks to a twelve year old girl's Random Act Kindness.

* * * * * * * * * * * * * * * * * *

A young lad gets a chance to shine

....

Billy Cable was standing outside a chain link fence. His fingers were entwined in the wires.

He was watching some of his pals inside that fence at a Pop Warner football practice.

He was wishing that he could be joining them, but his family couldn't afford the fee that was charged to join, so that put him on the outside looking in.

He understood, he was that kind of boy. But he would vision himself in the pads and uniform of a football player. If only.....

Sitting in the bleachers, watching the practice, was Bob Jacobs, a father of Jim Jacobs, one of Billy's close friends.

He noticed Billy at the fence on the other side of the field and wondered why he wasn't in there as well.

Must remember to ask his son about that.

The coach of the Pop Warner team, the Cowboys, was Sam Pringle, an associate of Bob Jacobs.

Perhaps he should be the one to ask.

At work the next Monday, Sam and Bob were having lunch and Bob asked about the little guy and why he wasn't among the others. He had noted that the boy looked every bit the part of a future football star.

Sam told him the reason and that Billy's parents were going through a tough time and just couldn't afford the fee.

Bob started to rub his chin in deep thought. He knew just exactly what he had to do.

Bob thought he knew Billy's father. He believed his name was John and that he worked at the car dealership where he had bought his last car.

Turns out he was right.

He wanted to approach him with an offer to pay Billy's fee to join the team, but didn't want to take the chance of embarrassing him.

He, instead, looked up the business manager for the league and made arrangements to pay, not only this year's fee, but future fees, if necessary.

The only condition was that no one was to know about it.

The business manager notified Billy's family that the league had decided to waver any fee associated to join the team. He made it sound as though the league would do that from time to time.

Billy was to join the team, the Cowboys, at their next practice.

Smart move.

The Cowboys went on to win the league and then go on to play in the Pop Warner Super Bowl and Billy Cable was the main reason as he turned out to be exactly what Bob Jacobs had predicted.

The future would see Billy go on to be an All American at state and on to a successful Pro career.

All because a caring father committed a Random Act of Kindness.

* * * * * * * * * * * * * * * * * * * *

A soldier's final award

....

Josh Bitner was a decorated veteran of the Korean War. (Police action, as it was called)

A *disabled* veteran, at that, because of the wounds he suffered in that conflict

He was well into his eighty's and living on a meager disability pension that barely covered his basic living expenses. There was never any money left for any pleasures.

He had no family to speak of and was visited only occasionally by a few elder members of the church community.

His greatest pleasure was watching sports on an ancient television that only got local TV stations. Cable or satellite television was out of the question.

One day, Isaac Washington, a member of the local pro basketball team had heard a story about a lonely veteran and how he was confined to his little world with nothing but an old television set and a few mementos of his past. He learned that he had received the Silver Star as a hero and that it seemed that no one cared for him.

Two days later, a couple members of the team showed up at his abode carrying a box that contained a cutting edge large screen television and cable box.

They were welcomed in and installed those items as Josh watched in wonder.

When he asked what that was all about, he got no answer; just wide smiles.

Then to top that, one day some team members stopped by, loaded Josh and his wheel chair into a van and drove him to the local arena.

There he was put on the side lines and got to witness one of his favorite sports right there out in front of it all.

When the game was over and they went to help Josh to the van, they noticed that he was slumped over in his wheel chair.

Sadly, he had passed.

However, everybody noticed there was a wide smile on his silent face.

A somewhat happy ending all because of a Random Act of Kindness on behalf of an incognito benefactor.

****

A lady didn't consider herself old

....

May Leland was a feisty lady in her nineties.

She had been raised, and spent her entire life, on a farm. That's probably how she had gotten to the ripe old age she enjoyed. 'Enjoyed' here is probably just an expression at this point.

She had a cozy, nicely decorated apartment, a

cat and quite a number of friends, both elderly and of younger generations. She was always a fun person to be around.

Boy, could she talk! Of course with her long life, she had a lot to talk about.

People loved to hear about the olden times and she could spin quite a few yarns of interest.

One day she was doing something she should not have been doing, fell, and broke her left hip.

Unfortunately, she lay where she fell for quite some time before anyone had found her

She was rushed to the local hospital and underwent an emergency hip replacement surgery.

That, of course, slowed her down for a number of weeks, and by the time she spent recovery time and therapy in local facilities, her apartment and especially her cat gotten neglected.

With so many friends, it was assumed by all of them that someone else was surely taking care of things for her.

Such was not the case.

One day, Dana Henderson, one of the friends, suddenly realized that, just perhaps, nothing was being done in that respect.

As it turned out, Dana was one of her friends

that knew where a key to her apartment was hidden and finally stopped by to check it out.

What she found was a half dead cat and some mail, mostly utility bills and such that had been slipped through her mail slot in the door.

First thing she did was take the cat to the vet and luckily the poor animal survived no worse for wear.

Then she gathered the unpaid utility bills and made sure they got paid.

From that point, Dana kept vigil on May's apartment and her cat.

After several weeks, came time for May to return home and she found everything pretty much as it was when she left.

She, or anyone else, never questioned or asked about it.

Dana never told anyone that it was she who had done the chore, but felt good about herself.

That was her Random Act of Kindness for this year.

* * * * * * * * * * * * * * * *

Mother-in-law to the rescue (?)

....

Sandra and Tom Zachman had been married for a little over ten years.

It was a good marriage by all standards. They were as deeply in love today as they were from the day they were married. Possibly, even more.

Problem?

Sandra's mother Vivian. She was always a take charge type that wasn't satisfied until every one around her thought the same way she did. Translate that to 'Control Freak'.

Sandra tolerated her, but with Tom, it was a different story.

There wasn't actual hate between them, more like tension.

As far as Vivian was concerned, Tom could nothing right.

"Never could see what Sandra saw in that man," she would often say to anyone who would listen to her.

However, if you looked down deep, You would see that Vivian didn't really feel that way about Tom. She just wanted to keep on top, so to speak.

She actually admired him for his intelligence and the way he treated her daughter and her grand children.

Of course, she would never let on about that.

Tom's work place was in turmoil. There was friction among employees and especially between Tom and his immediate boss.

It came to a head one day when Tom's boss told Tom to pack up his stuff, he was fired!

Word got to Vivian is a big hurry.

Several days later, one of the big bosses called Tom and told him to come in to see him on Monday morning.

Tom did just that and was told that the immediate supervisor that had fired him had, himself, been let go and that he, Tom, would now take his place.

Tom wondered, but did not question it. Only relished it.

Vivian was at their house when Tom got home that afternoon and told everyone the good news.

Vivian just smiled and didn't say a word

Tom looked at her with suspicion. "Why was she smiling and not saying anything. Wasn't at all like her," he thought, but what the heck.

What Tom, and Sandra for that matter, didn't know was that Vivian was a major stock holder in the company and a word or two from her got everything straightened out, big time.

It wasn't until Vivian passed that Tom and Sandra found that they had inherited Vivian's stock and realized she owned most of the company Tom worked for.

That now made sense about that episode at work a while back.

Her mother had pulled off fairly significant Random Act of Kindness.

* * * * * * * * * * * * * * * * * * * *

A pet is returned

....

Lester and Alma Kingston were on their way to their favorite camping area in the Rim Country.

The area was the most beautiful in all of Arizona as it over looked the lower basins to the south.

It seemed that you could get a different aspect of the view as the day would pass and the sun would paint yet another artistic awe inspiring site.

It was a view made famous by Zane Grey many years ago.

They were originally from Ohio and most of their camping trips were in the many camp grounds and lakes in Michigan.

Even though the families never know each other at that time, it was possible that they had run into each other.

Lester and Alma would eventually find each other and marry.

They and their three children, keeping up the tradition, have camped across country during their lifetime.

They were now retired and were free to come and go as they pleased and whenever they pleased.

Most of the campers in and around the camping area where they were, had RVs or trailers, the Kingstons had the same tent they had been using for years

It was patched and a bit thread worn at places but they wouldn't change if for anything in the world

It was sort of a lean-to type with a canvas tarp as a patio cover held up by poles.

They had their old trusty green Coleman stove and lantern that used white gas as fuel. It was getting hard to find that fuel these days,

One morning, Lester staggered out of the tent to

prepare the coffee and start the bacon frying. The odor from those two items floating in a wooded atmosphere was something to behold.

As he stepped out, the first thing he noticed was the dog that way lying next to the end of the picnic table.

It was a chocolate Lab that appeared to be just past the puppy age.

The dog sat up and gave Lester a look with a tilted head.

Lester said, "Well, what have we here?"

The dog looked back at Lester and if you could read its mind, it would probably be asking the same question of him.

He went over to the dog and held out his hand palm up, of course, so the dog wouldn't think he was going to hit it.

The dog hesitated a bit but finally made up to him.

"Where did you come from?" he asked the dog.

The Lab welcomed his behind the ear scratching and started wagging its tail,

By this time Alma came out to see who Lester was talking to.

"Aw," she said and went over to the dog and patted it on the head.

"Probably belongs to one of the campers around here. Hope it…or he," Lester said as he looked down and it became obvious the dog's gender, "knows where he belongs. Seems like he might be a precious member of some family."

"I wonder if we should feed him?" Alma asked, not to anyone in particular.

"Don't see any harm in it," Lester answered.

 The dog was looking at both of them and if you could, again read its mind, you would hear 'feed me! feed me'!

After the breakfast and the clean up, Lester and Alma got on their hiking boots to start on a trail they had wanted to explore.

When they started, the dog walked along with them as if it was expected.

They noticed that he was waging his tail so obviously enjoying the hike and the company

Lester and Alma weren't too sure about this because there had to be some family that must be missing their dog.

Never the less, they let the dog accompany them as they enjoyed the three or four mile hike – each way.

After the hike, they both hoped that the dog would go back where he had come from.

The Kingstons always stayed over until Monday morning because of the less traffic and they didn't have any schedule to follow.anyway.

When Lester got up that morning and went out of the tent, there was dog as if he was waiting for him.

"Oh no!" he thought as he looked around the camp ground and noticed that every body else had left, probably last night.

He called Alma out and showed that the dog was still there and asked, "What do we do now?"

Alma answered, "We certainly can't just leave him here."

"Looks like we had better take him home with us and do some detective work to find out who he belongs to," Lester said holding his chin and looking down at the dog.

The dog was waging its tail as if it knew what the conversation was all about.

The Kingstons returned to their home and the dog ran into their house ahead of them as if he belonged there.

It went from room to room checking out the surroundings, perhaps trying to find somewhere in the house that he could call his territory. Or perhaps he was looking for his owners.

The Kingstons took the dog to a vet to see if perhaps it had an embedded ID chip, but none showed up.

They called the local pond and the local animal shelter to see if anyone had been inquiring about a lost dog

Still no success.

They put ads in the local newspaper as well as some of the surrounding town newspapers with hope they might find the owners.

So far nothing worked and it looked as though the Kingstons might have a new member of their household.

Jimmy and Suzy Bottorff and family had been camping at that same campground at the same time as the Kingstons.

From the sadness in the family, it was obvious that the found chocolate Lab, "Hershey" was indeed theirs.

They were all beside themselves because "Hershey" had been in their family since a very small puppy, about a year and a half ago.

As it turned out, Bob Bottorff worked in the same accounting office as Sam Kingston, who was Lester and Alma's son.

Since they were in different departments, they only knew each other by sight and name only.

One day Sam overheard a conversation in the lunch room about Bob's family's lost dog.

He immediately put two to two together (after all he was an accountant) and figured the dog in question, no doubt was the dog that his parents had found.

He got Bob Bottorff's address and passed it on to his parents.

The next day, Lester, Alma and "Hershey" were walking up the Bottorff's walk.

They sat "Hershey" down on the porch, rang the door bell and stepped aside where they wouldn't be seen.

Both Jimmy and Suzy opened the door and there was a heart rendering welcome.

It looked as though Hershey's tail would break off from wagging so hard.

Jimmy and Suzy didn't notice Lester and Alma hiding behind a bush.

Bottorff's never knew who had returned "Hershey".

As the Kingston's drove away, the both gave a 'thumbs up' to each other.

* * * * * * * * * * * * * * * * * * *

A passenger gets help

Helen Brigham's telephone was ringing.

She was expecting the call, but dreaded it..

Her brother was calling with a message about her ailing father.

"Bad news, Sis," he was saying, "the doctors have given dad a very short time, perhaps not even through the night."

She figured that was the news she was dreading.

"I'm going to check out an airline ticket for you, and will let you know what I come up with," he told her.

Helen was glad her brother was going to take care of that for her because she really didn't have any idea how to go about it, let alone have the money to pay for it.

An hour later her brother called back, "Ok," he said, "but problem. I could only find one airline that could get you back here to Toledo in time, and the flight is booked up. You will be on stand-by and hope for the best.

Helen quickly packed up the few things she would need for the trip and had a neighbor drive her to the airport.

When she arrived she did the usual check in and through the security screening, then went to the gate counter.

The news wasn't too good. Seems there were quite a number of people on the stand-by list and her name was far down on that list.

She tried to explain her problem to the counter agent, but was told there wasn't too much she could do, but would try to do their best.

Standing Close by was Pamela Whitmer. She couldn't help hearing and felt sorry for the poor girl.

Pamela and her husband Ryan were first class passengers and when she went to the first class lounge, she told Ryan what she had heard.

That bothered both of them because they were compassionate People.

Pamela called the concierge over and asked if he would check into it for her.

A while later, he returned with the complete story. How this girl needed to get back to Toledo in time to visit her father who was apparently on his death bed.

Pamela then gave him some instructions....

The counter agent called Helen to her counter and told her that a seat became available and gave her a new ticket (round trip) and boarding pass.

Came time for boarding and every one walked down the passageway and into the plane.

Helen was looking at her boarding pass when a hostess asked if she needed help.

The hostess looked at the pass and directed her to the first class seating area.

Turned out to be across the aisle from Pamela and Ryan.

Helen was curious, but sat down to where she was directed. She looked over at the smiling Whitmers and smiled back

A little while after the plane took off, the Hostess came around to get order for drinks and food.

When she came to Helen, Helen explained she really couldn't afford anything.

"All complimentary," the hostess explained.

Helen was now really wondering about all this. Didn't make sense to her, but she would try to figure it out when her thinking gets back to normal.

Helen got back to Toledo in time to visit her father for the last two days of his life.

She never knew who had made that all possible.

The Whitmers had committed an act of kindness when it really mattered .

* * * * * * * * * * * * *

Author's notes:

The Random Acts of Kindness you have just read were, for the most part, fictional.

Lets hope that some of them, or some similar, actually did occur.

There really are a lot of kind people in this world

Donna and Arnie Gilson

ABOUT THE AUTHORS

Donna and Arnie Gilson are retired persons living in the pine forest surrounded town of Payson in what is known as the Rim Country or Arizona

www.ingramcontent.com/pod-product-compliance
Lightning Source LLC
Chambersburg PA
CBHW070502290526
45790CB00003B/1066